It's Not Too Late!
Making the Most of the
Rest of Your Life

(Third Edition)

Max Malikow

It's Not Too Late! Making the Most of the Rest of
Your Life (Third Edition)

Library of Congress Control Number: 2014932367

ISBN 9780991481101

To Tracy Brown: Who knows the value of each day.

To Diane Coville: Whose kindness is a blessing to all who know her.

To Rachel Joy Goodman: Who has inspired me to make the most of the rest of my life.

To Rabbi Dr. Earl A. Grollman: Who long ago saw something others did not see.

To Marvin Malikow: Who lived well.

To SC: Whose decency, faith, self-discipline, and wisdom have made her life exemplary.

Other Books by Max Malikow

Being Human: Philosophical Reflections on Psychological Issues

Living When a Young Friend Commits Suicide: Or Is Even Thinking About It
(Co-authored with Earl A. Grollman)

Philosophy 101: A Primer for the Apathetic or Struggling Student

Philosophy Reader: Essays and Articles for Thought and Discussions (editor)

Profiles in Character: Twenty-Six Stories that Will Instruct and Inspire Teenagers
(editor)

Suicidal Thoughts: Essays on Self-Determined Death
(editor)

Teachers for Life: Advice and Methods Gathered Along the Way

The Human Predicament: Towards an Understanding of the Human Condition

Preface

The best time to plant a tree is twenty years ago; the second best time to plant a tree is today.

- Chinese Proverb

When the English novelist George Eliot wrote, "You are never too old to be what you might have been," she made something of an overstatement. If you are sixty years old, it is too late to have a baby, win an Olympic gold medal, or graduate from medical school. Nevertheless, with the exception of goals that require youth, you are not too old to be what you might have been. Eleanor Roosevelt said, "In the long run, we share our lives and we share ourselves. The process never ends until we die. And the choices we make are ultimately our own responsibility."

There is an adage among ministers that when a preacher points to the congregation, there are three fingers pointing back at the one doing the preaching. Several years ago, Shannon Briggs won the heavyweight championship of the world by knocking out Sergei Liakhovich in the last second of the last round of their fight. Until that knockout –

literally at the last second – Briggs was losing the fight. As a baby boomer exhorting other baby boomers to keep punching until the final bell, I feel three fingers pointing at me. As you read the pages that follow, be mindful of the words of George Eliot and Eleanor Roosevelt and the example of Shannon Briggs.

Max Malikow
Syracuse, New York
August 25, 2013

Table of Contents

Introduction (Keyword: Persevering)

May you live all the days of your life.
                                    - Jonathan Swift

It ain't over 'til it's over.

                                    - Yogi Berra

One of the most successful coaches in sports history is Red Auerbach of the Boston Celtics. In addition to having been a brilliant strategist, he had a keen eye for basketball talent. When scouting a college player, Auerbach paid particular attention to how the prospect played in the closing minutes of a one-sided game. The coach reasoned that a player who continued to play hard after the game's outcome had been decided was the kind of player he wanted on the Celtics. A football coach of the same era, Vince Lombardi of the Green Bay Packers, maintained, "We never lose, we just run out of time." Both of these coaches understood the value of perseverance – playing hard until the end of the game.

If you're a baby-boomer (between the ages of 50 and 70) and picked up this book because of the title (*It's Not Too Late!*) it suggests that you have the quality of perseverance. Statistically, you have lived longer than you are going to live. You realize that from now on each successive day is a greater percentage of the rest of your life and you are determined to make the most of the time remaining. This determination implies persistence.

Psychologist Erik Erikson theorized the elderly reflect on their lives by asking the question, "Am I satisfied with how I have lived?" He characterized those who are able to answer, "yes" as approaching death with integrity. In contrast, he considered those who answer, "no" as approaching death with despair. The Hebrew word *shalom* is commonly understood to mean "peace." Actually, *shalom* has a richer meaning than mere absence of conflict. It means integrity in the way Erikson used the word. True *shalom* is the inner peace that comes from the confidence that one's life has been lived well.

Sir Thomas More is a striking historical example of *shalom*. Before imprisoned by Henry VIII for refusing to take the oath of approval of the king's divorce of Catherine of Aragon, a representative of the king appealed to More to affirm the oath. The official reminded More that all the other members of the court had declared approval of the divorce. "Thomas, take the oath," urged the official, "if not out of conviction, then join us for the sake of fellowship.

More replied, "And when you have died and gone to heaven for having done your conscience and I have died and gone to hell for not having done mine, will you join me in hell for the sake of fellowship?"

Whatever your age and current circumstances, picking up this book suggests that you believe *shalom* is a possibility for you. This is a book about discovering and making. Chapters two through four invite you to discover (or rediscover) three things that will enrich your life in the years ahead. Chapters five through seven direct you to make three things that will add meaning, pleasure, and satisfaction to the rest of your life. The result of all of this discovering and making will be true *shalom*. Nine other verbs that are integral to this book are presented as keywords at the start of each chapter: assessing, connecting, contemplating, deploying,

3

equipping, pacifying, persevering, planning, and reflecting.

The ideas in this book are not presented as tasks to be accomplished sequentially. Your mission, should you decide to accept it, will be to integrate into your life any combination of these six suggestions that have the potential to enhance the quality of your life. Although several of these upgrades can be made simultaneously, you will benefit from accomplishing any one of them.

Twenty-five centuries ago Socrates said, "The unexamined life is not worth living." He believed the best possible life is one that is lived thoughtfully. Deliberating on how to make the most of the rest of your life might be the biggest favor you can do for yourself. This book is intended to guide you in your deliberation.

I. Necessary Losses - Judith Viorst (Keyword: Assessing)

If you can dream and not make dreams your master.
                                          - Rudyard Kipling

Some people believe that holding on and hanging in there are signs of great strength. However, there are times when it takes more strength to know when to let go – and then to do it.
                                          - Ann Landers

You've got to know when to hold 'em, know when to fold 'em, know when to walk away, and know when to run.
                          - Kenny Rogers, "The Gambler"

Thirty-five years ago Judith Viorst challenged readers to assess their dreams and assumptions in her bestseller, *Necessary Losses*. Subtitled *The Loves, Illusions, Dependencies, and Impossible Expectations that All of Us Must Give Up in Order to Grow*, she advised those of middle-age to reconsider their dreams and relinquish those that will never come true. Viorst wrote that to cling to unfulfillable dreams will result in disappointment, distraction, and resentment. People who obsess over the things that might have been but never will be are nurturing discontentment and indignation. Further, their attention is drawn away from those things that are available for enjoyment.

One of the characters in W.B. Kinsella's ingenious novel, *Shoeless Joe*, is Archibald "Moonlight" Graham, a doctor who once aspired to be a major league baseball player. Good enough to have made it to the major leagues for only one inning of one game, eventually he went on to medical school and became the admired and beloved general practitioner in a small town in Minnesota. In a conversation he is told, "It's a tragedy you were a major league baseball player for only five minutes."

"No," the doctor corrected, "it would have been a tragedy if I had been a doctor for only five minutes."

It was necessary for him to give up one dream in order for another dream to come true. Psychologist Daniel Levinson has written of, "liberating yourself from the tyranny of the dream." Rabbi Harold Kushner teaches that a healthy response to the death of a dream is, "Let me try a new dream." Giving up an unfulfillable dream in order to reach a goal that is attainable includes the sadness that comes with the acceptance of reality. Journalist Richard Cohen knows about accepting an unfortunate reality. He is blind and living in a body that is continually deteriorating from multiple sclerosis. He has chosen not to lament the loss of his health and the activities that are no longer available to him. Instead, his focus is on being a husband, father, and writer. In his memoir, *Blindsided*, he wrote:

> I must rise above the culture of perfection and remember that I can be even if I can no longer do. I am learning to acknowledge weakness, accept assistance, and discover new forms of self-definition. ... A new male ideal will have to do and might even save me. I cannot allow myself to be held captive by old dreams.

In stark contrast to Richard Cohen is the bitter, elderly woman in Colleen McCullough's *The Thornbirds*. Mary Carson, a wealthy, once beautiful woman, is passionately in love with a man who is unavailable to her. He is a Catholic priest, wed to the church and half her age. Lamenting the loss of her beauty and obsessing over the man she cannot have, she declares her love for Father de Bricassart:

"I have loved you," she said pathetically. "No, you haven't. I'm the goad of your old age, that's all. When you look at me I remind you of what you cannot do because of age." "You're wrong. I have loved you. God, how much! Do you think my years automatically preclude it? Well, Father de Bricassart, let me tell you something. Inside this stupid body I'm still young – I still feel, I still want, I still dream, I still kickup my heels and chafe at restrictions like my body. Old age is the bitterest vengeance our vengeful God inflicts upon us. Why doesn't he age our minds as well?" She leaned back in her chair and closed her eyes, her teeth showing sourly, "I shall go to hell, of course. But before I do, I hope I get the chance to tell God what a mean, spiteful, pitiful apology of a God He is!"

Richard Cohen has chosen to assess his life in terms of what he has; Mary Carson has chosen to obsess over what she cannot regain (her youth and beauty) and have (Father de Bricassart). Theologian Dennis Prager has spoken of the missing tile syndrome in which eyes are drawn to the one missing tile in an otherwise perfectly laid ceiling.

One of human nature's most effective ways of sabotaging happiness is to look at a beautiful scene and fixate on whatever is flawed or missing, no matter how small. This tendency is easily demonstrated. Imagine looking up at a tiled ceiling from which one tile is missing – you will most likely concentrate on that missing tile. In fact, the more beautiful the ceiling, the more you are likely to concentrate on the missing tile and permit it to affect your enjoyment of the rest of the ceiling.

Aron Ralston's decision to focus on what remains after a loss saved his life. Trapped in a cave for five days when an 800-pound boulder shifted and pinned his arm against the cave's wall, he realized he would have to sacrifice his arm in order to save his life. When contemplating this unique self-surgery, Ralston imagined the life he would have as a one-armed man. He determined with the exception of playing the piano, he would be able to do with one arm all the things he previously enjoyed. His motivation came in part from considering what he would retain after the loss of his arm.

Randy Souders offers another impressive illustration of what remains after a loss. A quadriplegic since the age of seventeen as the result of a diving accident, Souders described his post-accident life, "like being ripped from one body that worked and placed in another one that didn't." Showing extraordinary self-discipline, he resolved to pursue the one thing his paralysis did not take from him.

> Near the end of my stay in the hospital one of my therapists almost forcibly strapped a paintbrush to my hand. The therapists had seen some of the things I'd done prior to my injury, and I was encouraged to paint. I found that I still had this little spark of artistic ability left. So it was almost like a big weight had been lifted. At least I could do something worthwhile again, and it became a vital part of my recovery.

Today Randy Souders is a successful artist with over 1,500 galleries that have displayed his work. One of his reflections is this paradox: "In a strange way, an injury like this, while it greatly complicates your life, also simplifies it." Having lost so much as a quadriplegic, he was forced to focus on what he could do if he was going to have a life of self-sufficiency and satisfaction.

A fundamental teaching of Buddhism is to accept that anything that is good and brings happiness is temporary. Richard Cohen, Aron Ralston, and Randy Souders are not Buddhists but have accepted that the fully functioning bodies they once had never will be again. They are in a position to be appreciative of what they once had and grateful for what remains available to them. Mary Carson is embittered by the loss of her youth and beauty – two conditions no one can keep. Her resentment prevents her from being grateful for what she once enjoyed. Further, her bitterness has blinded her to whatever might be a source of pleasure in the present.

A dictionary definition of gratitude is, "a feeling of thankful appreciation for favors and benefits received." Martin Seligman, a Professor of Psychology at the University of Pennsylvania and past President of the American Psychological Association, has studied the human condition for over thirty years. One of his research discoveries – and there have been many – is gratitude is a prerequisite for overall contentment with life. In *Authentic Happiness* he wrote, "Gratitude amplifies the savoring and appreciation of the good events gone by."

If grateful people are more likely to experience life satisfaction then it is worth asking: How is an attitude of gratitude acquired? The answer is grateful people choose to frame their lives positively and optimistically. Framing refers to how you choose to think about your life and describe your circumstances. Of course, the framing must be realistic. The man who fell out of the window on the twentieth floor of a building, reached the tenth floor on the way down, and said, "So far, so good!" is optimistic, but also unrealistic.

Grace and mercy are theological terms and in religious discussions they are characterized as two sides of the same coin. Grace is understood as an unearned, unmerited benefit; mercy is understood as a deserved punishment withheld. It is difficult, if not impossible, to assess your life and not see both unmerited favor received and merited punishment not dispensed. This is one way to frame your life in such a way that an attitude of gratitude is nurtured.

Another way to foster gratitude would be to keep a diary for two weeks in which you record the things for which you are grateful as they come to mind. You will then recognize the contributions of grace and mercy to your life. Further, you will see that framing your life positively has a mood elevating effect. Consider this exercise a non-pharmaceutical antidepressant: Every recovering alcoholic is familiar with Reinhold Niebuhr's *Serenity Prayer*: "God grant me serenity to accept the things I cannot change, courage to change the things I can and wisdom to know the difference." To know the difference between what you can and cannot control is to recognize your sphere of influence. To invest time, energy, or other resources on matters over which you have no control guarantees frustration and discouragement.

The ability to accurately assess one's sphere of influence is not only a life skill, but for some it was necessary for their survival. John McCain, Jeremiah Denton, Bob Shumaker, and James Stockdale are but four of many Vietnam War P.O.W.'s who attribute their survival and retention of sanity to having deployed their attention and effort only to those things that were within their control. Since it was not up to them as to whether or not they would be fed or tortured, they did not obsess over those possibilities. Instead, if fed, they could decide how to eat – all of the food at one sitting or a little bit at a time to make it last throughout the day. If tortured, they could say nothing for as long as possible or disclose meaningless information. (McCain once gave his interrogators the names of the Green Bay Packers' offensive lineman.

In Omar Kyayyam's "The Rubaiyat" is the following fatalistic analysis of life:

> 'Tis all a Chequer-board of Nights and Days
> Where destiny with men for Pieces plays:
> Hither and thither moves, mates, and slays,
> And one by one back in the Closet lays.

The psychological term for the perception that chance or outside forces determine our fate is *external locus of control*. It is undeniable there are many events and conditions beyond your control that impact your life. However, those who embrace the belief that they are pawns in the game of life and have no more influence on their fate than a ping pong ball going over Niagara Falls are likely to suffer depression. Psychologists call this passive resignation *learned helplessness* and it is the inevitable result of an *external locus of control*. Like Eeyore, the phlegmatic donkey in the Winnie the Pooh stories, the lament of those who have learned helplessness is, "What's the use?"

In contrast to the hopelessness of fatalists are those who believe they significantly control their destiny. These are people who have an *internal locus of control*. Psychologist David Myers, author of The *Pursuit of Happiness: Who Is Happy and Why*, has written: "In study after study, 'internals' achieve more in school, act more independently, enjoy better health, and feel less depressed than do 'externals.'

Aristotle's *Principle of the Golden Mean* characterized virtue as the apex between two extreme vices. Niebuhr's *Serenity Prayer* expresses a healthy balance and provides sane counsel. The survival stories of P.O.W.'s demonstrate that ideas have consequences and framing makes a difference.

II. Discovering (or Rediscovering) Flow (Keyword: Deploying)

People often say that this or that person has not yet found himself. But the self is not something one finds; it is something one creates.

- Thomas Szasz

His last name reads like an ophthalmologist's eye chart: Csikszentmihalyi. His book was a national bestseller in 1990: *Flow: The Psychology of Optimal Experience.* His research added a new word to psychology's vocabulary: *Flow* is a completely involved, focused state of consciousness, with diminished awareness of self and time, resulting from an optimal engagement of one's skills.

Defined prosaically, flow is experienced when time passes without notice because of engrossment in an activity. *Chronological time* is the same for everyone: sixty seconds in a minute, sixty minutes in an hour, twenty-four hours in a day. *Emotional time* is how the passing of time is experienced. On a long drive, it is children's heightened sensitivity to the passing of time that makes them ask, "Are we there yet?" In contrast, author Amy Tan can be so absorbed in writing that a month can go by before she realizes she has not spoken to anyone. Two people watching the same movie or sporting event will experience time differently depending on their interest in and enjoyment of the activity.

There is also a diminished sense of self-consciousness in flow. For Dan Keplinger, painting is a flow activity. Born with cerebral palsy, his continuous muscle spasms make routine tasks like talking, eating, and dressing arduous and frustrating. On his knees, he paints on a canvas laid on the floor, using a brush that protrudes from a headpiece. The self-proclaimed "King Gimp," (gimp means "soaring spirit"), Keplinger has said that when he is painting he is not aware of his body - the body that multiplies the difficulty of every ordinary operation. He has learned the truth of the Trappist monk Thomas Merton's words, "Art enables us to find ourselves and lose ourselves at the same time."

Consider the intensity of experience that is required to enable Dan Keplinger to transcend his body. (The Greek word from which the English word "ecstasy" is derived means "out of the body.") For him, this intense experience is painting. What is your flow activity? If you are not certain, perhaps these words of Csikszentmihalyi will be helpful:

> We have all experienced times when, instead of being buffeted by anonymous forces, we feel in control of our actions, masters of our own fate. On the rare occasions that it happens, we feel a sense of exhilaration, a deep sense of enjoyment that is long cherished and that becomes a landmark in memory for what life should be like. ... Contrary to what we usually believe, moments like these, the best moments in our lives, are not the passive, receptive, relaxing times – although such experiences can be enjoyable, if we have worked hard to attain them. The best moments usually occur when a person's mind or body is stretched to the limits in a voluntary effort to accomplish something difficult and worthwhile.

When have you been exhilarated by voluntarily stretching your body or mind to its limits in order to accomplish something worthwhile? The answer to this question is your flow activity.

Csikszentmihalyi deserves full credit for having coined the term flow. However, the concept of immersion in an activity with transcendence over time and ego has a long and varied history. Nearly a century ago the Syrian poet Kahlil Gibran wrote in *The Prophet*:

19

When you work you are a flute through whose heart the whispering of the hours turns to music. ... And what is it to work with love? It is to weave the cloth with threads drawn from your heart, even as if your beloved were to wear that cloth.

Reflecting on the Hindu Law of Dharma, Deepak Chopra wrote: "When you're expressing that one unique talent that you possess ... the expression of that talent takes you into timeless awareness."

Siddhartha Guatama, the Buddha, taught that one of the eight paths to be pursued in life is the path of right livelihood. What is right livelihood? It is work that brings benefit to both one's self and others. The benefit to the self is the fulfillment that comes from the utilization of talents and skills in work that one finds interesting.

Right livelihood is also indirectly addressed in Christianity. In Saint Paul's letter to the Ephesians he encouraged believers by describing them as uniquely created by God with gifts that are perfectly suited for their life's calling. Christian missionary and Olympic gold medallist Eric Liddell expressed his understanding of this when he said, "God made me fast and I can feel His pleasure when I run."

It's Not Too Late! Making the Most of the Rest of Your Life

Although not a Christian – and that is an understatement – philosopher and author Ayn Rand wrote, "I cannot recall a time when I did not know that I would be a writer." Perhaps the ultimate expression of a talent is the reflection of the tenor extraordinaire Enrico Caruso when he lamented, "All of my life I have been told that I have a great voice, but it is my great voice that has me." To consider yourself as the mere conduit of a gift is to recognize your flow activity.

The question for you is not, "Can you run like Eric Liddell; write like Ayn Rand; or sing like Enrico Caruso?" The question is, "What are you doing when you are unaware of the passing of time and unconscious of yourself?" Locate the activities, or at least one activity, in which you engage enthusiastically. Be mindful the word enthusiastic derives from the Greek words en (in) and theos (god). Jonas Salk, the medical researcher who developed the first successful polio vaccine, observed, "Happy is he who finds the God within and pursues it."

III. Discovering (or Rediscovering) Self-Discipline (Keyword: Equipping)

What lies in our power to do, lies in our power not to do.

-Aristotle

Ultimately, the only power to which a man should aspire is that which he exercises over himself.

- Elie Wiesel

Greater is he who ruleth his own spirit than he who taketh a city.

- Proverbs

Self-discipline is the ability to get yourself to do something you ought to do when it ought to be done whether you feel like it or not. The renown biologist Thomas Huxley thought so highly of self-discipline that he believed it to be the primary purpose of education. The all-time best selling self-help book, Scott Peck's *The Road Less Traveled*, is a three-hundred page teaching on the benefits of self-discipline. Another bestseller, Daniel Goleman's *Emotional Intelligence*, presents self-discipline as one of the five characteristics necessary for personal and professional success. In which of your life's accomplishments do you take the most pride? Did it require self-discipline? Likely, it not only required self-discipline but your exercise of self-discipline is one of the reasons why you are proud of that accomplishment.

It is also likely that your proudest accomplishment required planning. A bit of bumper sticker wisdom is *a failure to plan is a plan to fail*. Reconnecting with your proudest accomplishment will remind you that self-discipline and planning have served you well in the past. Making the most of the rest of your life will require a goal – something to be accomplished. As with your past accomplishments, self-discipline and planning will be necessary. Equipped with a plan and resolved to exercise self-discipline, you can meet any realistic goal.

Next, to determine your goal, ask yourself this question: What do I really want? The word *really* is an important part of this question. Whatever you want must be of value to you and realistic given your present circumstances. When answering this question do not ask too little of yourself. Be mindful that ninety year-olds have completed college degrees and seventy year-old runners have finished the Boston Marathon. (Johnny Kelley ran his last Boston

Marathon in 1992 at age eighty-four.) More remarkable than George Foreman regaining the heavyweight championship of the world at forty-five or forty-eight year-old Julio Franco of the New York Mets hitting a home run is sixty-four year-old Diana Nyad. A marathon swimmer, she swam 110 miles from Cuba to Florida - an endurance feat that took fifty-three hours. Equally impressive is Sensei Keiko Fukudo's accomplishment. At ninety-eight she achieved judo's highest level - a 10th degree black belt (the first woman to do so).

Really should also guide you in determining what you truly value at this time in your life. Do you desire reconciliation of a relationship? Is there a charitable cause to which you want to contribute? Do you have a story to tell that could be told as a book? (Note: Writing a book demands extraordinary self-discipline and planning.) Psychiatrist Irvin Yalom has written eloquently about the most haunting, provocative question a therapist can ask: "What do you really want?" Taken casually, this question will have no effect. Taken seriously, this question can determine the course of the rest of your life because, as Thomas

Merton wrote, "You are made in the image of what you desire."

The practice of psychotherapy can be understood as something that is very complicated or very simple. A simple explanation of the process is that it consists of two questions followed by a decision. The first question is: *What do you really want?* Asking yourself what you really want has implications for your thoughts and actions. This is the kind of investigation Socrates had in mind when he said, "The unexamined life is not worth living." The second question is: *Are your current thinking and acting getting you closer to or farther from what you really want?* If the answer to this question is, "farther," then the decision to be made is which are you going to change: what you want or your thinking and acting? Change does not come easily. Psychologist Albert Ellis speculated on the difficulty of change and why people resist the effort:

> The main reason people stay in jobs they hate, relationships that are abusive, friendships that are critical, and continue to smoke and drink excessively is low frustration tolerance – things must be easy. They say to themselves, "Even though it's desirable for me

to change in the long run, it's going to be very
hard in the short run, and therefore I'll do it
tomorrow, I'll do it tomorrow, I'll do it
tomorrow."

The other reason for procrastinating about
change is fear of failure. "If I change, I must
have a guarantee that it will work out, everything will be fine, I will succeed, and people
will love me. Since I don't have that guarantee, particularly in a new situation, I'll do it
tomorrow, or I won't do it at all."

Through the years in various courses I have
assigned students a behavioral change project. This
assignment calls for two brief papers. The first,
written in the first week of the course, requires the
students to describe a behavior they want to change
– something they either want to stop or start doing.
This paper must include a rationale for the behavior
they chose and a strategy for making the change.
The second paper, turned in at the end of the seme-
ster fifteen weeks later, calls for a progress report
and description of what they learned about change in
general and themselves in particular. Having read
hundreds of these papers through the years, I have
noted a pattern in the second assignment. The
students' reflections can be categorized into one of
four conclusions, all of which begin with the letter R.

Resignation: The comedian Steve Allen said, "I am loyal to a fault. I have many faults and I am loyal to all of them." Some of the students concluded that the change was beyond their capability and resigned themselves to a lifelong habit they did not want or a desired behavior they will never have.

Reevaluation: Other students reported that upon further consideration, their selected change is something they really did not want after all. These students believed they were capable of change but miscalculated the importance of the behavior they chose. Without the conviction that the behavioral change would enrich their life, they lacked the incentive to persevere and succeed.

Rationalization: A few students reasoned that it was good that they did not succeed at changing. In contrast to those who resigned or reevaluated, these students argued that the behavior they thought they wanted to change actually served them well. Rationalization is the construction of self-justifying explanations in place of the real and unconscious reasons for one's actions. In other words, rather than admitting to a lack of self-discipline or weakness of the will, these students formulated self-satisfying, comforting explanations.

Repentance: Even fewer students – approximately ten percent - succeeded in their effort at change. They reported a behavioral "about face." (The Greek word *metanoia*, which is translated into the English word repent, is a marching term meaning "turn around and walk the other way.") These students wrote that they were pleasantly surprised by the satisfaction they experienced from their success. They also reported satisfaction from having exercised self-discipline and enhanced confidence in their ability to make other changes in the future.

IV. Discovering (or Rediscovering) Who Your Friends Are (Keyword: Connecting)

The only man who behaves sensibly is my tailor; he takes my measure anew every time he sees me, whilst all the rest go on with their old measurements, and expect them to fit me.

- George Bernard Shaw

The sad sack comedian Rodney Dangerfield often complained, "I've got to make some new friends." The phrase *bad friends* is an oxymoron. In *Ordering Your Private World*, Reverend Gordon MacDonald makes the distinction between VDP's (Very Draining People) and VEP's (Very Energizing People). A similar distinction is made in Scott Peck's *The People of the Lie* in which he characterizes some people as *biophilic* and others as *necrophilic*. The former love contributing to the growth and development of others; the latter derive pleasure from diminishing and discouraging others.

The story of Job found in the Hebrew Bible is a narrative of suffering. Job is the object of a cosmic wager in which God allows Satan to orchestrate events that bring unspeakable pain into Job's life. At the apex of his suffering he is visited by three friends (Eliphaz, Bildad, and Zophar) who have come to be referred to, sardonically, as "Job's comforters." Tormented by disease, financially ruined, and emotionally depleted by the deaths of his ten children, Job's three very draining visitors erroneously explained his misfortune as God's punishment for egregious sins. They relentlessly exhorted Job to confess his wrongdoing and argued that he had been punished in proportion to the severity of his misdeeds. Actually, Job was a righteous man who maintained his faith in God in spite of these tragedies. If ever there was a man who needed to make new friends it was Job.

While bad friends is an oxymoron, *good friends* is a redundancy - unless good means especially close. One of the qualities of a good friend is optimism. When the author Tony Hendra was fourteen he had an affair with a married woman. When this tryst was discovered he was taken to a priest for counseling. The priest was a Dominican monk named Father Joe, who became a lifelong friend and mentor to Hendra. One of Father Joe's characteristics in this

relationship was his optimism concerning Hendra and
his future.

Kay Jamison is a brilliant psychologist who for
years was plagued with manic-depression and suicidal thoughts. Her psychiatrist balanced a realistic
assessment of her illness with an optimistic view of
her potential. In her superbly written memoir, *An
Unquiet Mind*, she wrote of him:

> He made it unambivalently clear that he
> thought I had manic-depressive illness and
> that I was going to need to be on lithium,
> probably indefinitely. ... I respected him
> enormously for his clarity of thought, his ob-
> vious caring, and his unwillingness to equivo-
> cate in delivering bad news. ...He was very
> tough, as well as very kind. ... He treated me
> with respect, a decisive professionalism, wit,
> and an unshakable belief in my ability to get
> well, compete, make a difference.

In addition to optimism, good friends are good
listeners. Singer and songwriter Gordon Lightfoot's
"Rainy Day People" includes these lyrics: "Rainy day
people don't talk, they just listen 'til they've heard it
all." A radio advertisement for the Mormon Church
that encourages family communication includes a
brief skit in which a daughter says to her mother,

"Mom, if we talk will you be quiet?" Sweetly, the mother responds, "I'd love to."

Hendra's Father Joe was an exceptional listener. After Father Joe's death, Hendra visited the monastery and told one of the monks that Father Joe made him feel like he was the only person in the world when they spoke. The monk responded, "I know, he made all of you feel that way." Hendra learned that Father Joe met and corresponded with hundreds of people, including the late Princess Diana. He was such a good listener that he never spoke about himself or any of the other people to whom he ministered. Good listeners like Father Joe give you their undivided attention.

The description of love found in the New Testament is beautifully simple and simply beautiful. Located in 1 Corinthians 13, it is frequently used as a reading in marriage ceremonies. One of the fifteen characteristics of love enumerated in this passage is that love "is not self-seeking." This is also one of the qualities of a friend.

Several years ago in a marriage counseling session with an especially contentious couple, the wife said of her husband, "He doesn't even know the meaning of the word love."

In an effort to inject a bit of levity into the situation I said to the husband, "You've been charged with not knowing the meaning of the word love. How do you plead?"

"Not guilty," he responded, "I certainly do know the meaning of the word love."

The definition he gave was exquisite and I have used it ever since. An engineer, his definition of love reflected his marvelous analytical mind. He said, "Love means always being committed to the best interests of another apart from one's own."

Before I could compliment him on his definition, his wife, obviously unimpressed, blurted, "See! I told you he doesn't know the meaning of love."

Her husband's definition was an elaborate expression of love not being self-seeking. Further, it agreed with a well-known precept of moral philosophy. The eighteenth century German philosopher Immanuel Kant taught that people should never use other people to achieve something for themselves. He reasoned that since nothing is more valuable than a human being, no one should ever be used or sacrificed to advance someone else's interests. Kant believed that people should never be considered as a means to an end – especially someone else's selfish end.

Empathy is the ability to identify with the feelings of another person. It has been characterized as the ability to become another person, to a certain extent, for a little while. There is a difference between feeling sorry for someone and feeling with someone. The former sentiment is sympathy; the latter is empathy. Good friends are empathic.

Earlier in this book a reference is made to Daniel Goleman's bestseller *Emotional Intelligence*, in which he posits that there are five personality traits that correlate with personal and professional success. Empathy is one of these traits. The ability to accurately assess what another person is feeling; locate that feeling in your own experience; and respond to that person appropriately are necessary for effective, satisfying relationships. Goleman believes that without relational skills, personal and professional success are nearly impossible.

Physician Edward Rosenbaum learned empathy the hard way. Without realizing it, for years he had been practicing as an empathically challenged doctor, insensitive to his patients' anxiety and fear. It was not until he was diagnosed with laryngeal cancer and became a patient himself that he acquired an appreciation for the helplessness and uncertainty experienced by his patients. His story is told in the aptly titled book, *A Taste of My Own Medicine*. (Dr. Rosenbaum's story was also made into a movie, "The Doctor," starring William Hurt.)

Professor Betty Sue Flowers has written, "Pain is a mechanism for growth. It carves out the heart to make room for compassion." Friends reach into their own experiences of pain, thus enabling them to have unfeigned compassion for those who are suffering. In his classic memoir, *Man's Search for Meaning*, psychiatrist and Holocaust survivor Viktor Frankl wrote that while it is unfortunate that pain is an inevitable part of life it can be put to good use. Like Flowers, he believed that pain generates compassion. He further believed that when people show compassion, they not only bring comfort to others but they alleviate their own suffering as well. This reciprocal benefit is the concept that Father Henri Nouwen had in mind when he chose *The Wounded*

Healer as the title for his book on pastoral care and counseling.

A fifth characteristic of friends is that they are unconditionally accepting. Unconditional acceptance is a term that is subject to misunderstanding. It is not approval of anything and everything people do. It is recognition of the value of all people in spite of anything they have done. Such acceptance is rare, but worth pursuing according to Father Nouwen:

> We probably have wondered in our many lonesome moments if there is one corner in this competitive, demanding world where it is safe to be relaxed, to expose ourselves to someone else, and to give unconditionally. It might be very small and hidden. But if this corner exists, it calls for a search through the complexities of our human relationships in order to find it.

In Victor Hugo's *Les Miserables* an escaped convict, Jean Valjean, steals silverware from the rectory of a priest who has extended hospitality and kindness to the fugitive. When Valjean is apprehended, the priest arranges for the thief's release, allows him to keep the silver, and implores him to use the money from the sale of the silver to start a new life as an honest man. This demonstration of

unconditional acceptance proves to be a life changing
experience for Valjean.

In contrast, the psychoanalyst Alice Miller has
written eloquently of the damage done by parents
who conditionally accept their children:

> It is one of the turning points in analysis when
> the narcissistically disturbed patient comes to
> the emotional insight that all the love he has
> captured with so much effort and self-denial
> was not meant for him as he really was, that
> the admiration for his beauty and
> achievements was aimed at this beauty and
> these achievements, and not at the child
> himself. In analysis the small and lonely child
> that is hidden behind his achievements wakes
> up and asks: "What would have happened if I
> appeared before you, bad, ugly, angry,
> jealous, lazy, dirty, smelly? Where would your
> love have been then? And I was all these
> things as well. Does this mean it was not
> really me whom you loved, but only what I
> pretended to be? The well-behaved, reliable,
> empathic, understanding, and convenient
> child, who in fact was never a child at all?
> What became of my childhood? Have I not
> been cheated out of it? I can never return to
> it. I can never make up for it. From the
> beginning I have been a little adult. My
> abilities – were they simply misused?

Shakespeare wrote: "Those friends thou hast
and their adoption tried, grapple them to thy soul

with hoops of steel." Discovering or rediscovering who your friends are and connecting or reconnecting with them means you will choose to spend your time and share yourself with empathic people who are engaged listeners, optimistic about you, and accept you unconditionally.

V. Making a Realistic List of Things to Do Before You Die (Keyword: Planning)

You'll always miss 100% of the shots you don't take.
- Wayne Gretsky

The biggest temptation is to settle for too little.
- Thomas Merton

In *Blood Brothers* Michael Weisskopf recounts his experience as an embedded reporter in Iraq. The time he spent recovering from his wounds was a time of reflection. His *Time* magazine article, "How I Lost My Hand But Found Myself," is the story of a sixty year-old man focused on what he does and does not want to do with the rest of his life.

Michael Weisskopf lost his hand; Aron Ralston lost his arm; and Randy Souders lost his fully functioning body. Each considered what he wanted from the rest of his life and determined to play the hand he had been dealt. For professional boxer Billie Miskie the rest of his life was only a couple of months. A contender who had fought the great Jack Dempsey for the heavyweight championship of the world in 1920, three years later Miskie's health was rapidly evaporating from kidney disease. Financially broke but determined to celebrate his last Christmas with his family, he arranged for the fight he knew would be his last. Remarkable is that he got out of a sickbed to show up for the fight. Miraculous is that he won the fight, a four round knockout of Bill Brennan in Omaha, Nebraska. The $2,400 Miskie earned provided gifts for his wife and three young children as well as a sumptuous Christmas dinner. Billie Miskie died exactly one week later in a Minneapolis hospital.

Of course, you could question his decision, which almost certainly hastened his death. You could question how he chose to spend his last paycheck. Those decisions notwithstanding, there is no disputing that Miskie was decisive about what he was going to do with the rest of his life.

In stark contrast to Billie Miskie's decisiveness is the ambivalence of J. Alfred Prufrock. "For all sad words of mouth or pen, the saddest are these: 'It might have been," wrote John Greenleaf Whittier. The haunting speculation of what might have been is presented in T.S. Eliot's poem "The Love Song of J. Alfred Prufrock." Lonely and middle-aged, Prufrock

vacillates over whether or not to declare his love for
the woman he fears might see him only as a friend.
Each time he resolves to tell her how he feels, his
fears of rejection and humiliation overwhelm him and
he procrastinates. His indecisiveness is captured by
the poet with the reflection that there is time yet,
"For decisions and revisions, which a minute will
reverse." Prufrock's procrastination extends to the
end of his life and he grows old wondering, "Would it
have been worth it all?"

David Rakoff, celebrated for extraordinary wit,
departed from his usual style and reflected on fear
when he was diagnosed with cancer:

> Fear lays waste to one's best reserves. It fo-
> ments rot in my stores of grain, eats away at
> my timbers. If I dwell on the possibility that I
> might be dead by forty-seven, I can't really
> find a useful *therefore* in that. Therefore, I
> will train for the marathon, confess the long
> unspoken torch for X, etc. (Fear) just leaves
> me frozen; amotivated and stunned.

Elisabeth Kubler-Ross is well known for her
work in the field of death and dying. Her research
resulted in the discovery of the five stages experienced by terminal patients: *denial, anger, bargain-*

ing, depression, and *acceptance*. The last of these stages is characterized by the patients' resolution to get their affairs in order. Getting affairs in order means finishing unfinished business and includes things like making final contact with certain people, completing important tasks, and making a trip that has been long postponed. It could include doing something capricious. One man, who said he always wanted to go to the airport and take the next departing plane regardless of where it was going, finally acted on that whim.

There is a lesson to be learned from terminal patients. Imminent death has a way of facilitating the separation of what is important from what is not important and identifying the things that ought to be accomplished. Samuel Johnson wrote, "When a man knows he is to be hanged in a fortnight, it concentrates his mind wonderfully." In the previous chapter reference is made to Viktor Frankl's instruction to make optimal use of life's three inevitable tragedies (pain, guilt, and death). He wrote the awareness of the brevity of life can be used advantageously. Rather than lamenting that life is a brief candle, Frankl proposed using that reality to motivate us to deploy our limited time on things that truly matter to us. While we might not be terminal patients, each of us has a temporary condition - life - and the clock is ticking.

A children's poem written by Marva Collins warns against procrastination and the insidiousness with which the years pass:

Mr. Meant-To

Mr. Meant-To has a comrad,
and his name is Didn't Do;
Have you ever chanced to meet them?
Did they ever call on you?
These two fellows live together
In the house of Never-Win,
And I'm told that it is haunted
By the ghost of Might-Have-Been.

The insightful Quaker philosopher Elton Trueblood believed people cannot find satisfaction in life unless they have the reassurance that their lives are transcendent in two ways: *self* and *time*:

> (A man's life) must transcend his own ego in that he cares more for a cause than for his own existence, and it must transcend his own brief time in that he builds for the time when he is gone and thereby denies immortality.

A legacy is that which is left behind for the benefit of others. Trueblood so strongly believed in the importance of a legacy that he considered it a necessary part of the meaning of life. In *The Life We Prize* he wrote: "A man has made at least a start on discovering the meaning of human life when he plants shade trees under which he knows full well he will never sit." Henri Nouwen showed agreement with Trueblood with these words: "When a man is no longer able to look beyond his own death and relate himself to what extends beyond the time and space of his life, he loses his desire to create and the excitement of being human."

Although a legacy is commonly thought of in terms of property and money, it can take other forms. A realistic list of things to do before you die should include making arrangements for leaving something behind that will bear your name and provide a benefit to others. For Billie Miskie it was a memorable Christmas. What will it be for you?

It is rare when inspiration can be drawn from a magazine advertisement. Yet, one automobile ad included this thought:

It's Not Too Late! Making the Most of the Rest of Your Life

Time cannot be influenced by mankind. It gives each of us a beginning, and an end. And this makes us question the significance of what comes in between. But if you can create something time cannot erode, something which ignores the eccentricities of particular eras or moments, something truly timeless, this is the ultimate victory.

You still have enough of this commodity called time to start creating or complete something to leave something behind that "time cannot erode." The British novelist Arnold Bennett reflected on this commodity and its uniqueness in *How to Live on Twenty-Four Hours a Day*.

Time is the inexplicable raw material of everything. With it, all is possible; without it, nothing. The supply of time is truly a daily miracle, an affair genuinely astonishing when one examines it. You wake up in the morning, and lo! Your purse is magically filled with twenty-four hours of the unmanufactured tissue of the universe of your life! It is yours. It is the most precious of possessions. ... No one can take it from you. It is unstealable. And no one receives either more or less than you receive. In the realm of time there is no aristocracy of wealth, and no aristocracy of intellect. Genius is never rewarded by an extra hour a day. And there is no punishment. Waste your infinitely precious commodity as much as you will, and the supply will never be withheld from you. ...

Moreover, you cannot draw on the future. Impossible to get into debt! You can only waste the passing moment. You cannot waste tomorrow; it is kept for you. You cannot waste the next hour; it is kept for you. I have said the affair is a miracle. Is it not?

VI. Making Peace With Your Past
(Keywords: Pacifying and Reflecting)

No man is rich enough to buy back his past.

- Oscar Wilde

Soren Kierkegaard wrote, "Life can only be understood backwards, but it must be lived forwards." Embroiled in World War II, Sir Winston Churchill expressed a similar sentiment when he said, "If we open a quarrel between the past and the present, we shall find that we have lost the future." Psychoanalysts believe in order for patients to resolve inner-conflict in the present they must achieve a thorough understanding of their personal history. To make the most of the rest of your life you will have to review your past, but not to the degree called for by psychoanalysts and certainly not at the expense of your future. Exploration of your past must be purposeful in a way that is obvious to you. Constructing a timeline of your life might prove helpful in getting started on your investigation and separating significant events from those that are irrelevant to your mission. Looking over photographs, leafing through your high school yearbook, and reading correspondence you have saved are provocative activities for reflecting on your past.

The past can be characterized the way some people speak of a vacation spot: "It's a nice place to visit but I wouldn't want to live there." Although making peace with your past is a separate chapter in this book, it could have been included in the previous chapter: "Making a Realistic List of Things to Do Before You Die." Making peace with your past will include at least two categories of forgiving and three types of learning. Forgiving will involve forgiving others as well as yourself. Learning will involve learning from your successes, failures, and misfortunes.

Forgiving Others

Philosopher Mike W. Martin has eloquently defined forgiveness:

> Forgiveness is the act of relinquishing or avoiding negative attitudes toward someone for a wrong they have committed. Distinct from the outward act of telling others they are forgiven, forgiveness is an inner act or activity; it is a change of heart from ill will (hatred, anger, or contempt) to good will. It need not

imply a complete acceptance of a person, nor a return to the same good relationship we had with someone. It does, however, open the door to a renewal or restoration of relationships.

Neither Professor Martin's definition nor Jesus' teaching to, "Forgive us our debts, as we forgive our debtors" provides instructions as to how to accomplish forgiveness. Forgiving is not easily done. It is no wonder that one skeptic wryly observed, "To err is human, to forgive is rare."

Forgiveness is a state of mind expressed by inaction. The state of mind is the result of the hard choice to neither resent someone nor desire misfortune for that person. The inaction is not pursuing punishment for an offense or payment for a debt. Moreover, forgiveness is not forgetting. If we could will to forget an injurious act it would be unnecessary to forgive. Forgiveness does not result in a clean slate such that an individual's prior behavior has no influence on future interactions. Jesus taught recurringly on forgiveness but also instructed on the importance of counting the cost when making decisions. He also instructed his disciples to "be as innocent as doves and wise as serpents."

It has been noted previously that forgiveness does not come easily. Nevertheless, it can be facilitated by reframing the offense committed against you. In chapter one the concept of framing is described as how people choose to describe their circumstances. If you have a nagging feeling of pain or anger or both when you think about how you have been wronged then it is likely that you will have to engage in reframing in order to exercise forgiveness. This is the challenge confronting Mack, the protagonist in William Paul Young's novel, *The Shack*. It is the story of a grieving father whose daughter, Missy, was abducted and murdered. Mack has an encounter with God, Who encourages him to forgive the murderer. God counsels Mack that he will be unable to accomplish this unfathomable forgiveness unless he reframes his understanding of the man who took Missy's life.

Each of the following strategies for reframing requires you to focus on yourself rather than the person you are considering forgiving. The first strategy is illustrated by a true story. Several years

ago in a town where I lived, a highly regarded
minister had a lapse in wisdom and morality and
committed adultery. (Aristotle said in sexual passion
people experience an eclipse of reason.) When the
minister's sin was publicly disclosed, those who
trusted and respected him were outraged at his
betrayal. However, one man, upon hearing of this
moral failure, paused and reflected. When this man
finally spoke he said, "I was just wondering if there's
ever been a time in my life when I could have
committed adultery." When weighing the forgiveness
of others, reframe what they did by asking if there
has been a time when you could have committed the
same sin. Do not be surprised if you find that same
offense lurking somewhere in your past. Adam
Morton has made a bolder assertion. In the
introduction to his book, *On Evil*, he posits that any
offense that cannot be located in our behavioral
history nevertheless resides within our capability:

> We're in the midst of it as always. Human be-
> ings are committing atrocities upon one
> another with the same enthusiasm or care-
> lessness that has always marked our species.
> When we think of evil we think of large scale
> horrors. ... By the end of the book I hope to

have convinced you that most evil acts are performed by people disturbingly like you and me.

Greek philosophers of old taught there are four virtues: temperance, justice, courage, and wisdom. It is likely that the sin against you resulted from someone's failure to exercise one of the so-called *Cardinal Virtues*. One way to reframe the offense against you is to ask yourself: Have I ever hurt another person by failing to practice self-discipline or fairness or courage or sound judgment?

Reducing the intensity of your anger toward someone is another way of facilitating forgiveness. Psychologist and author Wayne Dyer found that reciting the following question to himself usually mitigates his anger: *Why can't you be more like me?* This question brings him to realize the arrogance and foolishness of thinking he should be the standard for excellence in human behavior.

A third strategy for making forgiveness easier is to recognize that it would be good for you. In *Forgive and Forget* Lewis Smedes wrote:

> Carrying a grudge is a loser's game. It is the ultimate frustration because it leaves you with

> more pain than you had in the first place. Recall the pain of being wronged, the hurt of being stung, cheated, demeaned. Doesn't the memory of it fuel the fire of fury again? Do you feel that hurt each time your memory lights on the people who did you wrong? Your own memory becomes a videotape within your soul that plays unending reruns of your old rendezvous with pain. ... The only way to heal the pain that will not heal itself is to forgive the person who hurt you. ... When you release the wrongdoer from the wrong, you cut a malignant tumor out of your inner life. You set a prisoner free – yourself.

A fourth strategy for forgiveness is so simple that it was employed by a seven-year-old girl named Ruby Bridges. Her story became well known from the writing of the eminent child psychiatrist Robert Coles. When attending a psychiatric conference in New Orleans in 1962 he happened upon a riot outside an elementary school. Dr. Coles quickly realized this mob scene was a violent protest against the desegregation of this previously all-white school. At the center of this storm, escorted by federal marshals, was Ruby Bridges – the school's first black student. Curious about what she was experiencing as the target of insults and threats, Dr. Coles arranged to meet with her.

In his meetings with her he became impressed with her quiet strength and dignity. In one of their conversations he asked her about something she appeared to say to the mob when walking past them one morning. Ruby corrected him, saying, "I wasn't talking to them. I was talking to God."

"What were you saying to God?" asked Dr. Coles. Ruby explained that the crowd reminded her of a prayer and she prayed it. "Which prayer?" he asked.

Ruby responded, "Father, try to forgive these people, because they don't know what they're doing."

Amazed, Coles responded, "Ruby, why would you pray for people who frighten you and want to hurt you?"

Unfazed by his disbelief, she asked, "Well, don't you think they need praying for?"

Ruby Bridges lived up to a standard she set for herself. Religion at its best is when it is lived out with displays of charity, grace, and forgiveness. Ruby did not allow her code of conduct to be compromised by the cruelty of others. If, like Ruby, forgiveness is a virtue you have embraced, consider exercising it independently of the misbehavior of others. This is something you can do for yourself.

Forgiving Yourself

Boxing legend Muhammed Ali is a man who can forgive himself. Consider this description of himself as a young man:

> I used to chase women all the time. And I won't say it was right, but look at all the temptations I had. I was young, handsome, heavyweight champion of the world. Women were always offering themselves to me. I had two children by women I wasn't married to. I love them; they're my children. I feel just as good and proud of them as I do my other children, but it wasn't the right thing to do. And running around, living that kind of life, wasn't good for me. It hurt my wife, it offended God. It never really made me happy. But ask any man who's forty years old – if he knew at twenty what he knows now, would he do things different? Most people would. So I did wrong; I'm sorry. And all I'll say as far as running around chasing women is concerned, is that's all past. I've got a good wife now, and I'm lucky to have her.

If you think he is being too easy on himself, why? Do you have something in mind that he ought to do for atonement? In the previous chapter, one of the items on the list of things to do is finishing unfinished business. If Ali has expressed regret for his womanizing and apologized to the people he has hurt then he is in a position to forgive himself. Aristotle's ethical *principle of the golden mean* teaches that moral excellence is the apex between two extremes. In Muhammed Ali's case, one extreme would be denial that he did anything wrong or hurt anybody. Such denial would be sociopathic. The other extreme would be an obsession with his wrongdoing and a life of guilt, shame, and unforgiveness of himself culminating in his suicide. Between these extremes is where you find Ali − responsible, remorseful, and appreciative of his present circumstances.

The definition of forgiveness does not change when the person who is forgiven and the person who forgives are the same. It is still a change of heart from ill will (hatred, anger, or contempt) to good will. However, the strategies for self-forgiveness are somewhat different from those for forgiving others. When considering forgiving yourself, you would do well to ask yourself four questions.

(1) Have I ever forgiven someone else for the
same misdeed? When Jesus Christ was asked, "Which
of the commandments is the greatest?" he responded, "Love the Lord your God ... and love your neighbor as yourself." Applying his answer to self-
forgiveness means that you should extend to yourself
the same graciousness you have extended previously
to a neighbor you have forgiven.

(2) Why can't I be more like the person I want
to be? Perhaps you noted the similarity of this question to the one used by Wayne Dyer. The answer to
this question is: *There is no reason why you cannot
become more like the person you want to be.* If guilt
is inhibiting self-forgiveness then apply the teaching
of Viktor Frankl. He wrote that guilt should be employed as a tool to provoke you to resolve to do
better in the future by living up to the standard you
have set for yourself. Further, as with any tool, it
should be put away so that you will be able to find it
the next time you need it.

When asking yourself why you cannot be more
the person you want to be, also consider this: *You
are who you are most of the time.* It is probable that
the wrongdoing for which you need to forgive

yourself is not typical of you. Bill Buckner had a commendable career as a major league baseball player. Over twenty-two seasons he accumulated 2,715 hits including 174 home runs. He had a career batting average of .289, and won a batting championship. In addition, his career fielding percentage of .992 means that 99.2 percent of the ground balls, line drives, pop flies, and thrown baseball's intended for his glove were fielded without error. Nevertheless, he is associated with a single ground ball that eluded his glove in the 1986 World Series that arguably cost the Boston Red Sox their first championship in sixty-eight years. It's unfortunate as well as unfair that many Red Sox fans associate him only with that error. In like manner, rather than characterizing yourself in terms of your worst moment, forgive yourself for infrequent lapses in good conduct.

Psychologists David DeSteno and Pierre Valdesolo addressed the human penchant for giving disproportionate attention to the worst moments and behaviors of others. In *Out of Character* they ask, "Should a single moral failing erase a lifetime of good behavior? Why does a single transgression seem to give us license to brand someone with the indelible mark of a marred character?" In response to their own question they offer:

> One explanation is that because these single events are so shocking and so memorable (not to mention so beaten to death by the media), they eclipse all else. Why doesn't a single good deed, even a memorable one, ever seem to be seen as a mark capable of defining a person's true colors? Ever hear of Farron Hall, the homeless alcoholic who lived under a bridge in Winnepeg, who in May 2009 risked his own life by jumping into the Red River in a heroic attempt to save a drowning teen? ... he was patted on the back by local officials and quickly forgotten. In society's eyes, this one good act wasn't nearly enough to redeem Hall from a lifetime of "degenerate behavior." Rather than characterizing yourself in terms of your worst moment, forgive yourself for infrequent lapses in good conduct.

Another expression of who you are is what you do about what you do not like about yourself. The fact that you have disappointed yourself and resolved to change is not only commendable, it makes you forgivable.

(3) How does it serve anyone for me not to forgive myself? Can you think of anyway in which you or someone else benefits from you not forgiving

61

yourself? Conversely, can you think of any way in which you or someone else will be worse off if you do forgive yourself? If the answer to both of these questions is "no" then self-forgiveness should seem reasonable as well as practical.

(4) Like Ruby Bridges, do I believe forgiveness is a virtue? Virtue is moral excellence. If you believe that forgiveness is a virtue then you are practicing moral excellence whenever you forgive – including when you forgive yourself.

Learning from Success and Failure

In his classic poem, "If," Rudyard Kipling describes one of the qualifications for adulthood with these words: "If you can meet with triumph and disaster and treat those two impostors just the same." An impostor is someone who deceives by pretending to be someone or something else. Kipling was wise to use the word impostor to describe triumph and disaster because they seem to be permanent and definitive when actually they are temporary and indecisive. Triumph (success) and disaster (failure) intermittently yield to each other and neither defines who you are.

It's Not Too Late! Making the Most of the Rest of Your Life

Making peace with your past includes reflecting on both success and failure; enjoying the former and learning from both. It has been said a man who believes at fifty what he believed at twenty has not been paying attention. Recently, two of the world's wealthiest men met with students at the University of Nebraska College of Business Administration. In their presentation, Warren Buffett and Bill Gates shared with students some of the principles that have contributed to their extraordinary success as well as the value of learning from mistakes and failure.

Remember the title of this book is: *It's Not Too Late! Making the Most of the Rest of Your Life.* Planning your future requires an understanding of those things that have worked well for you in the past as well as those that have not and should be avoided. Whatever you consider a success must be something that had value for you. Whatever you value should provide some guidance for the deployment of your time and attention going forward. As for your self-evaluated failures, ask yourself what you miscalculated that resulted in falling short.

Learning from Misfortune

Learning from misfortune is not the same as learning from failure. Misfortune refers to situations and events you did not choose and cannot be attributed to mistakes you made. A misfortune is the hand you were dealt and challenged to play. When you reflect on misfortunes that have touched your life do not be surprised if you say what a Vietnam veteran once said about his experience of war: "I wouldn't trade it for a million dollars but I wouldn't give a dime to do it again." The legendary Alabama football coach Paul "Bear" Bryant was asked why he preferred a running game to a passing attack. "Because when you put the ball in the air," he explained, "there are three things that can happen (an incompletion, an interception or a completion) and two of them are bad." Consider the things that can happen in life and it might seem like most of them are bad: war, cancer, death of a loved one, financial loss from a natural disaster, loss of a job from corporate restructuring, loss of a limb from someone else's negligence, crime, mental illness, unavoidable bankruptcy, marital infidelity. (The ease with which this list was compiled was discouraging.) Is it any wonder Rabbi Harold Kushner's book, *When*

It's Not Too Late! Making the Most of the Rest of Your Life

Bad Things Happen to Good People, was a bestseller in 1981 and remains in print thirty years later?

Of her own depression the brilliant psychologist Kay Redfield-Jamison has written: "Depression is awful beyond words or sounds or images; I would not go through an extended one again." Yet, after describing with stunning eloquence her agonizing existence when depressed, she went on to write:

> So why would I want anything to do with this illness? Because I honestly believe that as a result of it I have felt more things, more deeply; had more experiences, more intensely; loved more, and been loved more; laughed more often for having cried more often; appreciated more the springs, for all the winters; worn death "as close as dungarees," appreciated it – and life – more; seen the finest and most terrible in people, and slowly learned the values of caring, loyalty, and seeing things through.

A novel by Elleston Trevor, *The Flight of the Phoenix*, is the story of a commuter plane that crashed in the desert. Although none of the crew or passengers were killed, the plane was mangled. Among the passengers was an aeronautical engineer who examined the wreckage and confidently proposed building a new plane from the remains of the old. What followed is a story of determination, inge-nuity, leadership, persistence, and teamwork. Making peace with your past probably will require examining some wreckage. Make the effort to reframe your misfortune, lest you see yourself as a victim and immobilized. Learning from misfortune involves surveying life's wreckage and taking an inventory of what remains that can contribute to a future project.

VII. Making a Philosophy of Life (Keyword: Contemplating)

Success is the ability to go from one failure to another with no loss of enthusiasm.
> - Sir Winston Churchill

And when you get the chance to sit it out or dance, I hope you dance.
> - Mark Sanders and Tia Sillers

The purpose of philosophy is not to think well, but to live well.
> -Timothy Luke Johnson

In chapter four a reference is made to Father Joe, a Dominican monk who was a friend and counselor to the author Tony Hendra. One of Father Joe's qualities that impressed Hendra was the monk's keen insight into the issues of life. Hendra wondered how this man, who had spent most of his adult life cloistered in a monastery, could have such wisdom about life and a profound understanding of a world with which he did not have direct contact. Father Joe's discernment came from his life of contemplation. While few are called to such a life, everyone can benefit from thinking about what philosophers refer to as the ultimate questions. These questions are ultimate because they comprise the foundation upon which people build a life.

An expression of these ultimate questions is the observation of the aforementioned Irvin Yalom. Sounding more like a philosopher than a psychiatrist, he maintains there are four life issues that permeate psychotherapy:

> (1) There is no apparent meaning to life.
> (2) We are responsible for the exercise of our free will.
> (3) We have simultaneous, conflicting needs to confess and keep secrets about ourselves
> (4) Eventually we are going to die.

According to Dr. Yalom, more often than not these issues are addressed indirectly and operate as four currents running beneath the surface of psychotherapy. One way of pondering his theory is to consider that people usually have some thoughts concerning these issues. Ask them about astronomy, archaeology, geology, or oceanography and if they have not given themselves to formal study of these subjects they will confess ignorance. Ask them if they believe in an afterlife; what they think about the meaning of life; or if they have any thoughts concerning free will and responsibility and they are likely to have something to say. The ultimate issues are pondered, with or without the aid of formal study, because without them there can be no philosophy of life. Without a philosophy of life there is no basis for decision-making.

Another way of testing Yalom's theory is to recall the thoughts you have had when attending a wake or funeral; taking responsibility for a misdeed or bad decision; contemplating a career change; or fearing that some secret about yourself has been discovered. These mundane experiences are familiar expressions of the ultimate issues.

Although this chapter's title is *making a philosophy of life*, a more accurate alternative would be *reflecting on and revising a philosophy of life*. Formulating a philosophy of life is analogous to an explorer making a map. In life and mapmaking, unexplored territory is traveled and charted with refinements made following further exploration. No one wakes up one morning and decides, "Today is the day I make a philosophy of life." As you prepare to make the most of the rest of your life, revisit and entertain revising what you believe about life's meaning, free will, responsibility, self-disclosure, and death. These deliberations will not be mere intellectual exercises. Your philosophy of life will influence you in discovering flow, assessing friendships, formulating a list of things to do, and making peace with your past.

Epliogue

The older I grow the more I distrust the famous doctrine that age brings wisdom.

- H.L. Mencken

Justice is one of philosophy's Four Cardinal Virtues. Nevertheless, I am glad that I live in a world in which justice is not perfectly administered. In a world of perfectly dispensed justice there would not have been many of the unearned good experiences and undeserved good people I have enjoyed. Granted, in a world of perfect justice no undeserved misfortune would have befallen me. However, on balance, more unmerited favor has come my way than random adversity.

Previously quoted are these words of Soren Kierkegaard: "Life can only be understood backwards, but it must be lived forwards." In seeking to understand your life by looking backwards, be open to the conclusion that on balance you have experienced more unearned good than undeserved bad. In looking backwards do not overlook the ordinary blessings that are often unrecognized. Oncologist Norwood Anderson observed, "When I think all of the things that could go wrong with a human body I consider good health a miracle." If you have had many years of good health count that as a favor rather than an entitlement. Beyond good health, if you consider all that could go wrong in life but did not go wrong for you, perhaps you will conclude that you have been blessed with a good life.

This book has directed you to plan for the final third or fourth of your life by reflecting on necessary losses, flow activities, accomplishments, friends, unfinished business, a legacy, forgiveness, success, failure, misfortune, and a philosophy of life. Twenty-five years after the liberation of the Nazi concentration camps, Holocaust survivor and Nobel laureate Elie Wiesel wrote: "A quarter century. And we pause, trying to find our bearings, trying to understand: what and how much did these years mean?" This book has encouraged you to look back and learn before moving forward.

Wisdom is the quality of having experience, knowledge, and sound judgment. It is accumulated over a lifetime and provides guidance for living life as it ought to be lived. Planning how to use the balance of your life will require wisdom. Mencken is correct in his observation that life experience alone is insufficient for wisdom. Wisdom comes with age only if it is accompanied by reflection on how the years have been spent and the beliefs that have guided that spending. Knowledge of how life ought to be lived mixed with how life has been lived is the formula for making the most of the rest of your life.

www.ingramcontent.com/pod-product-compliance
Lightning Source LLC
Chambersburg PA
CBHW050558280326
41933CB00011B/1893